Historical Atlases of South Asia,
Central Asia, and the Middle East

A HISTORICAL ATLAS OF

UZBEKISTAN

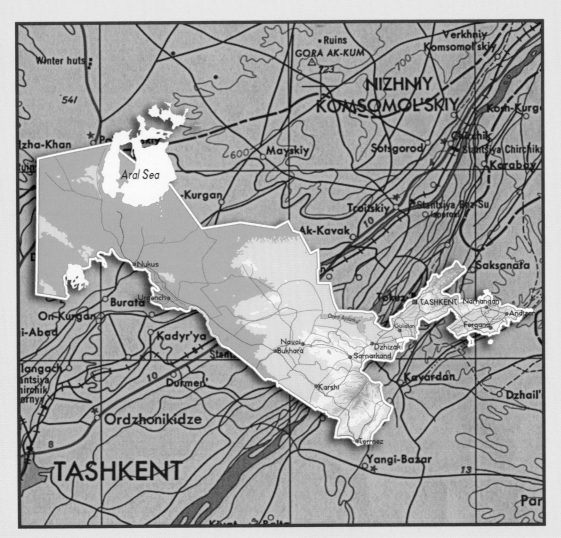

Aisha Khan

The Rosen Publishing Group, Inc.

To my parents, a constant source of inspiration and encouragement

Published in 2003 by The Rosen Publishing Group, Inc.
29 East 21st Street, New York, NY 10010

Library of Congress Cataloging-in-Publication Data

Khan, Aisha.
A Historical Atlas of Uzbekistan / Aisha Khan.
p. cm. — (Historical atlases of South Asia, Central Asia, and the Middle East)
Summary: Maps and text chronicle the history of the Central Asian country that became independent of the Soviet Union in 1991.
Includes bibliographical references and index.
ISBN 0-8239-3868-9
1. Usbekistan—History—Maps for children. 2. Uzbekistan—Maps for children.
[1. Uzbekistan—History. 2. Atlases.]
I. Title. II. Series.

G2168.31.S1 K4 2002
911'.587—dc21

20022031035 2002032143

Manufactured in the United States of America

Cover image: Uzbekistan *(modern map, center)*, its people *(bottom left)*, and its capital city of Tashkent *(U.S. Army map, circa 1957, background)* have been overcome throughout history by conquerors such as Timur, whose body rests in the Gur-i-Emir Tomb in Samarkand *(bottom right),* and influenced by modern leaders such as its current president Islam Karimov *(right),* pictured here in 2002.

Contents

INTRODUCTION

Uzbekistan is one of the five countries that make up Central Asia. The other four are Kazakhstan, Turkmenistan, Kyrgyzstan, and Tajikistan. The word "stan," common in the names of many Asian countries, means "land." Stan is a word that was adopted into several languages from ancient Persian. Uzbekistan means "the land of the Uzbeks," while Tajikistan means "the land of the Tajiks," and so on.

This may sound like a distinct division of people, but countries are rarely ever made up of only one kind of people. This is especially true for states in central Asia, where populations are multicultural, multilingual, and multiethnic. There are Tajiks in Uzbekistan, for example, and Uzbeks in Kazakhstan. There are also Russians, Germans, and even Koreans in these countries.

Uzbekistan—a landlocked country that was formerly a part of the Soviet Union—gained its independence in 1991 after being conquered by Russia during the late nineteenth century. A socialist republic since 1925, Uzbekistan has a rich political history of repression and rebellion. Now host to one of Central Asia's most authoritative governments, Uzbekistan keeps a watchful eye on its young populace—half of its 25 million citizens are under eighteen years of age—hoping to curtail the influence of radical fundamentalist Muslim groups in the region. Eighty-five percent of the population of Uzbekistan is Muslim.

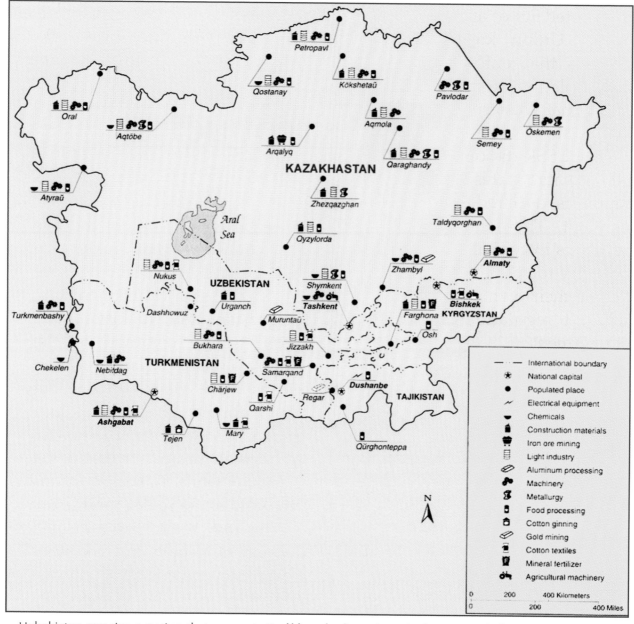

Uzbekistan remains a nation that supports itself largely through agriculture, mainly by exporting cotton. The country's natural resources have paid a costly price for its ongoing production, however. The use of pesticide chemicals such as DDT, as well as the depletion of the Aral Sea for the purposes of irrigation, has contributed to Uzbekistan's vast environmental problems. In 2002, Uzbekistan was the world's third-largest cotton exporter.

Russia, which headed the Union of Soviet Socialist Republics (USSR), which once controlled the region, first drew the borders that defined these states. The USSR created these states to strengthen its own hold over central Asia. During the Soviet era, not much was known about Uzbekistan. This was partly because of the Cold War hostility between the United States and the USSR. The Soviet Union kept international policies that enforced its secrecy and isolation from other nations, afraid that Western countries would attempt to weaken its government.

The USSR dissolved in 1991, and all of its states, called Soviet republics, declared themselves independent. These included the five republics in central Asia. They were now free to hold their own elections, decide their own policies, and exist without regulation by the Soviet government.

Recent developments in the region, especially in Afghanistan, have created a greater interest in central and South Asia. People want to know more about Asia's inhabitants, its history, and its culture. Western governments want to form alliances with Asian countries because of their strategic locations and rich natural resources.

Uzbekistan, which was the center of ancient civilizations, boasts the region's most historic towns, cultural achievements, and architectural splendors. For these reasons, Uzbekistan regards itself as one of the most important countries in central Asia and often takes a leading role in regional politics.

As its name suggests, Uzbekistan is primarily composed of Uzbeks, descendants of ancient Turkic tribes. The language spoken by Uzbeks is part of the Turkic group of languages. It shares similarities with the languages of the region's other Turkic peoples. In fact, the majority of people in central Asia trace their heritage to ancient Turkic and Mongol tribes.

For centuries, Uzbekistan has been the center of a cultural crossroads. Merchants from China, Persia (Iran), India, Arabia, North Africa, and Europe crisscrossed its land from ancient times, along trading routes later called the Silk Road. They carried silks from China and spices from India, and brought horses from central Asia to Rome and Greece. In return, civilizations along the Silk Road were influenced by distant cultures. Eventually, Greek philosophy, monotheistic religions, and various artistic styles influenced the land later known as Uzbekistan. Its cities, such as Bukhara, Samarkand, and Khiva—centers of cultural, intellectual, and economic development—attracted scholars and artisans. However, they also became targets of conquerors.

Over the centuries, Uzbekistan has been a part of many empires—Iranian, Greek, Chinese, Arab, Mongol, Turk—and its historical influences have contributed to its unique modern identity.

1 EARLY HISTORY

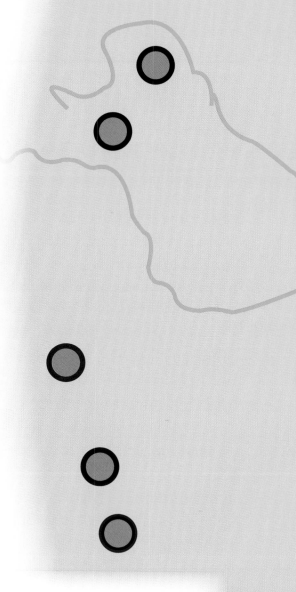

Geographically, historically, and culturally, Uzbekistan is the heart of Central Asia. It shares its borders with Kazakhstan, Turkmenistan, Kyrgyzstan, Tajikistan, and Afghanistan. It is a landlocked country, a little larger than the state of California, with a population of more than 25 million. Uzbekistan has 3,866 miles (6,221 kilometers) of land borders. It lies between two very important rivers, the Amu Darya and the Syr Darya, which have sustained life in the region for thousands of years. Northeastern Uzbekistan is part of the fertile Ferghana Valley.

Uzbekistan's terrain consists of grasslands known as the steppes, sandy desert areas, and lush river valleys along the Amu Darya, Syr Darya, and Zerafshan Rivers. In the east, mountain valleys surround the Ferghana

Historians now believe that the remains of farming settlements in the central Asian region now known as Uzbekistan date back at least 8,000 years. Scholars point to new evidence that shows that waterways such as the Amu Darya and Syr Darya, which empty into the Aral Sea, were once used to irrigate crops much like they do today. Stone Age tools have also been found along the shoreline of the Caspian Sea.

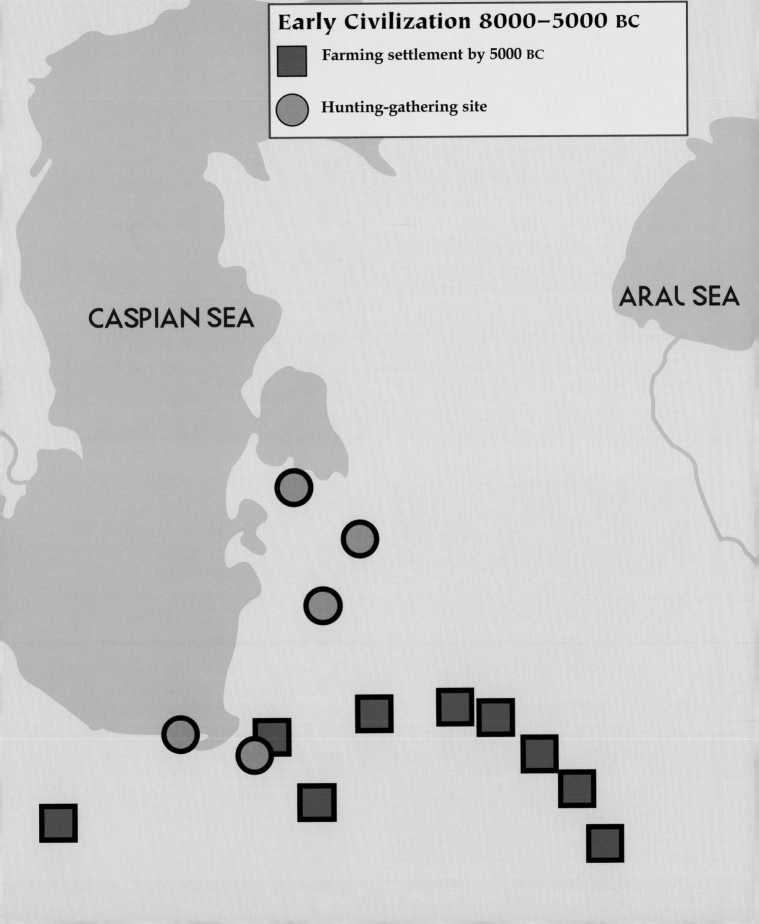

Early Civilization 8000–5000 BC

■ Farming settlement by 5000 BC

● Hunting-gathering site

CASPIAN SEA

ARAL SEA

Valley. In the north, Uzbekistan borders the shrinking Aral Sea. During ancient and medieval times, most of Uzbekistan was known by its Greek name, Transoxania.

According to archaeological evidence, humans have been living in central Asia for at least 100,000 years. Uzbekistan's earliest inhabitants were most likely nomads who roamed the vast grasslands in search of food. These nomads are believed to be the first humans to domesticate horses. With the domestication of animals, ancient peoples became more mobile. Horses helped people inhabit regions to the west, such as Turkey and eastern Europe, and eastern lands such as Mongolia.

Sarmatians: Amazons in Central Asia

Ancient Greek historians wrote of a ferocious group of tribes, rivals of the Scythians, known as the Sarmatians, famous for their women warriors. Hippocrates wrote that the women of the tribe had no right breasts. As babies, their right breasts were branded and cauterized (seared) so that they would not grow. This was believed to strengthen the right arm. The famous scholar Herodotus also wrote that Sarmatian women hunted on horseback with their husbands and fought in wars wearing the same dress as men. Archaeologists have found many female warriors in military burial sites, placed in a central position surrounded by gold, indicating their importance.

At the same time, people in some areas were making permanent settlements. All along the rich, fertile valleys of the Amu Darya and Syr Darya, in present-day Khwarezm, Bukhara, and Samarkand, people were establishing villages, as well as developing agriculture and irrigation systems.

In fact, the interaction between nomads and settlers has been the moving force of history in Uzbekistan and all of central Asia. Until the twentieth century, there

Although the Scythians had no written language, they were an advanced nomadic people who are credited as the first Asians to have domesticated horses, as shown on this fifth-century tapestry.

had been a constant cycle of migration, conquest, settlement, and new conquest. When nomads roamed the steppes in search of pastures for their animals, they occasionally raided settlements for food and supplies. Some people remained and settled down, while others moved on. This cycle continued over centuries, bringing new people and cultures into the oasis settlements.

The Scythians

By 800 BC, a distinct group within the central Asian nomadic communities had emerged. These nomadic tribes spread across the steppes from the Don River in the east to the Danube in the west. The neighboring Greeks called them Scythians, while the Persians (Iranians) called them Sakas.

A Greek historian, Herodotus, wrote accounts of the Scythians in the fifth century BC. Recently, archaeologists have discovered many burial sites rich with artifacts that provide more insight into these people. Ethnically, historians believe that the Scythians were related to the Indo-European (Aryan) group of peoples spread from Europe to India. The Scythians were hunters, and they survived on fish and game. They also drank horse milk rather than water. They loved gold, archaeologists believe, and used it to make ornaments and decorate household goods. The Scythians are believed to be among the first people to wear trousers, which made horse riding easier. Mostly a nomadic people, the Scythians did not rely heavily on

Able to survive in an extreme environment that was largely infertile, some Scythians eventually raised wheat, though most were seminomadic shepherds who wandered the steppes with their herds of livestock. This fragment of a saddle is just one example of Scythian artisanship. Besides their frequent use of gold to ornament their bodies, archaeological evidence now suggests that the Scythians were elaborately tattooed and often created saddles and harnesses that were uniquely decorated with colorful images of animals. They also fashioned leather and fabric clothing, including soft boots.

water the way other communities did. They did not even use it for bathing. Women covered themselves with a paste of herbs, which was left on their bodies overnight and removed the following day, leaving their skin clean.

The Scythians were famous for their skills in horseback archery and guerrilla warfare. They raided neighboring towns and kingdoms to gain wealth and capture loot. The Scythians reveled in these conquests. They were notorious for beheading their enemies and drinking from human skulls covered with gold.

Emergence of the Silk Road

By the fifth century BC, three great civilizations—Greek, Persian, and Chinese—encircled Transoxania. These highly developed kingdoms had established trade and diplomatic relations with each other. This led to the development of the Silk Road, the name for a number of routes leading from China and Persia to Greece and Rome. Merchants, ambassadors, and adventurers traveled these routes, the longest of which ran approximately 5,000 miles (8,047 kilometers). In the earliest days of travel, traders carried silk, a unique product produced only

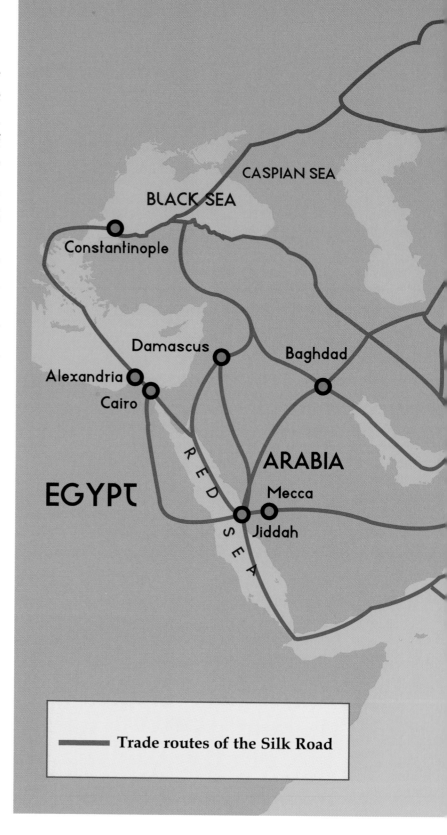

Trade routes of the Silk Road

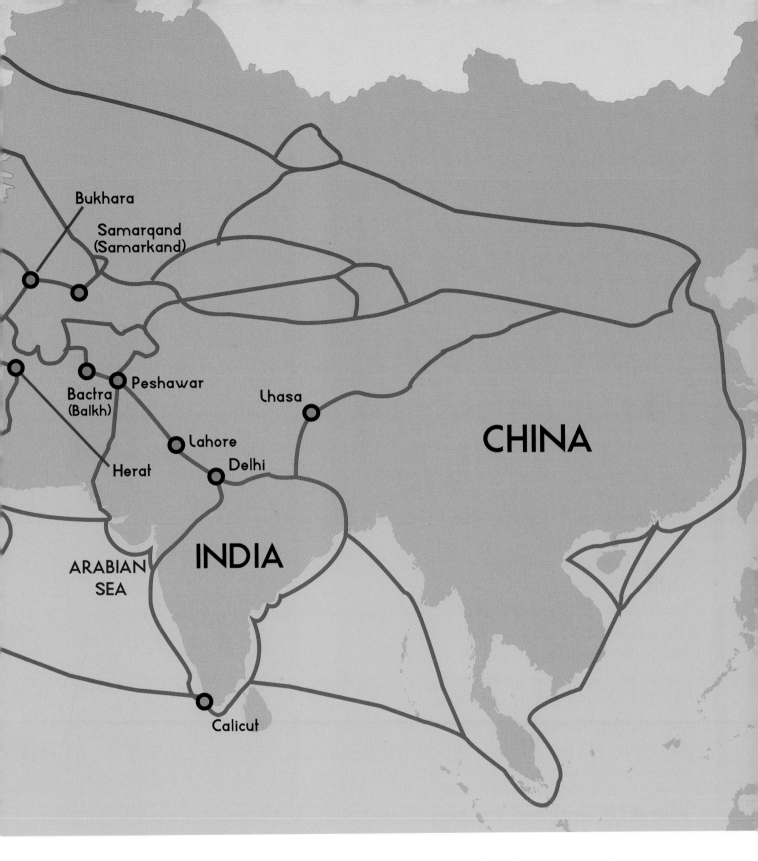

Bukhara

Samarqand
(Samarkand)

Bactra
(Balkh)

Peshawar

Herat

Lahore

Delhi

Lhasa

CHINA

INDIA

ARABIAN
SEA

Calicut

The Silk Road—a 5,000-mile/8,047-kilometer trade route that linked northern Asia with China and parts of Europe—made Bukhara and Samarkand profitable and therefore inviting to conquer throughout the centuries. Both cities—now part of present-day Uzbekistan—are known for remarkable Muslim architecture, with many structures covered in traditional blue tiles.

in China. These routes crisscrossed Transoxania, boosting trading practices that contributed to the development of Bukhara, Samarkand, and Sogdiana (Ferghana Valley) as centers of culture. This exchange of goods and information also spread religions such as Buddhism, Judaism, and Zoroastrianism throughout the region.

Zoroastrianism

Zoroastrianism is named after the Prophet Zoroaster (also called Zarathusthra), who preached around 6 BC in the Achaemenid Court. Zoroastrians worship an all-powerful god, Ahura Mazda, who is represented by fire. Their holy book is the *Zend Avesta*. Though identified with Persia, the religion probably originated in Bactria or Sogdiana. Today most Zoroastrians live in western India and are known as Parsees ("from Persia"), though there are also small communities of Parsees in Iran. The religion is often termed "dualistic," meaning it follows the belief in the struggle between two powers, good and evil, fighting constantly for control of the world.

The Achaemenid Empire

Around the sixth and seventh centuries BC, a Persian king, Cyrus the Great (600–529 BC), established the first world empire. It stretched from

Zoroastrianism, once a faith of the kings of Persia, was practiced in this Zoroastrian tomb built by Darius I to house the sacred flame. Followers of the religion, started by the Persian prophet Zoroaster (683–553 BC), were known to have worshiped fire, as a symbol of the original light of god, and Ahura Mazda.

Persia (Iran) to the Aegean Sea, encompassing Egypt, Syria, and much of south central Asia and Afghanistan. The Achaemenid Empire, as it was known, was constantly invaded by Scythian horsemen from the north who raided Persian towns and looted their wealth. The third Achaemenid emperor, King Darius the Great, fed up with Scythian raids, decided to conquer Transoxania. He pursued the Scythians for some time, as they retreated northward. Exasperated, Darius annexed the territories south of the Syr Darya in the fourth century. He divided them into three satrapies (dependent kingdoms)—Khwarezm, Sogdiana, and Bactria (now southern Uzbekistan, Tajikistan, and Afghanistan)—all owing allegiance to him. The Scythians continued the hold on their northern territories.

Persian influence led to a more settled lifestyle in Transoxania and the introduction of their state religion,

Zoroastrianism, to the region. While absorbing Persian influence, the Scythians maintained a distinct identity, which was erased only after the victorious sweep of the Macedonian conqueror Alexander the Great.

The Greeks

In the fourth century BC, Alexander the Great (356–323 BC), king of Macedonia, set out in his conquest of the known world. His main target was the mighty Achaemenid Empire, renowned for its wealth and culture. After successfully conquering not only Persia but also Egypt,

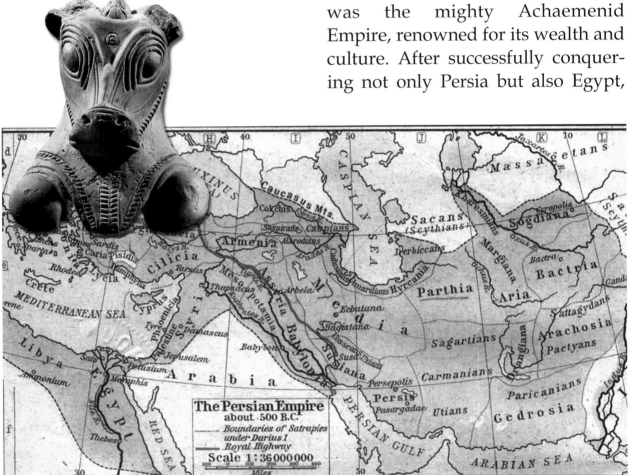

This 1923 map of the Persian Empire features its expanse under Darius I. Credited with uniting all the peoples that the Persians had conquered, including Assyrians, Phoenicians, Medes, Lydians, and Indians, Darius was regarded as a great administrator. Under his leadership, the empire was divided into satrapies (provinces) with separate leaders assigned to each. Inspectors working under his guidance would travel to each satrapy, instruct its leader, collect tributes (taxes), and examine its military strength. The Achaemenian sculpture of a bull's head (top left) can be traced back to the time of Cyrus the Great, the founder of the Persian Empire.

This detail of a sixteenth-century map by Abraham Ortelius was published as part of Parergon, now widely recognized as the first Western historical atlas. This image, which was once a part of Ortelius's *Theatrum Orbis Terrarum* (*Theatre of the World*), features Alexander the Great's expedition and conquests throughout Asia. Alexander's fleet is depicted as sixteenth-century ships, and the inset illustration shows a fantastic place where he went to answer the question of the future outcome of his expedition.

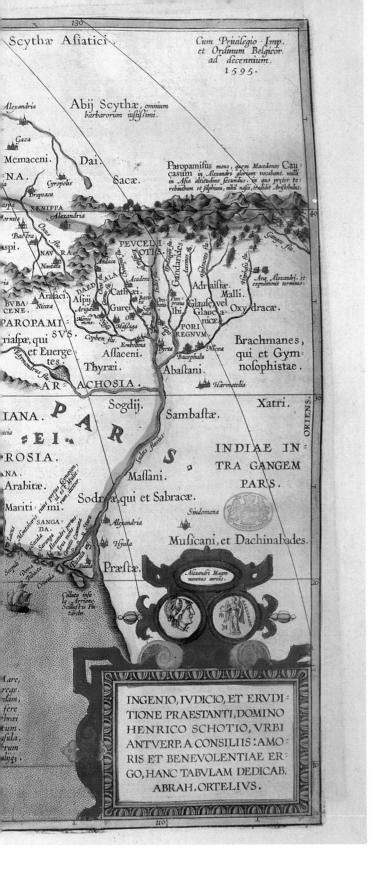

king, Darius III, had fled to Bactria, and Alexander pursued him there. However, before they could face each other, Darius was killed by his own men. In 329 BC, Alexander decided to move on to conquer the legendary city of Samarkand, which the Greeks called Macaranda. After taking Samarkand, Alexander defeated the Scythians north of the Syr Darya. Alexander established many cities in his name, including Alexandria (present-day Khojent) in Uzbekistan, which was the last of the seventeen cities founded by Alexander that bore his name.

Alexander stayed in Transoxania for two years, protecting his territory from several rebellions by Sogdian and Bactrian princes. By 327 BC, he had decided to move his armies through present-day Afghanistan toward India.

Alexander's victorious sweep through central Asia connected territories stretching from Egypt and Greece to India and China. It led to an infusion of Greek, Persian, and Asian cultures, sparking achievements in art, architecture, and literature. Alexander died in 323 BC at thirty-three years of age, before he could consolidate his victories. Afterward, his empire split into many satrapies ruled by Greek commanders. As a result of these territorial divisions, Seleucus took over

Syria, Mesopotamia (Iraq), and Byzantium (Istanbul), Alexander pushed farther east. The Persian

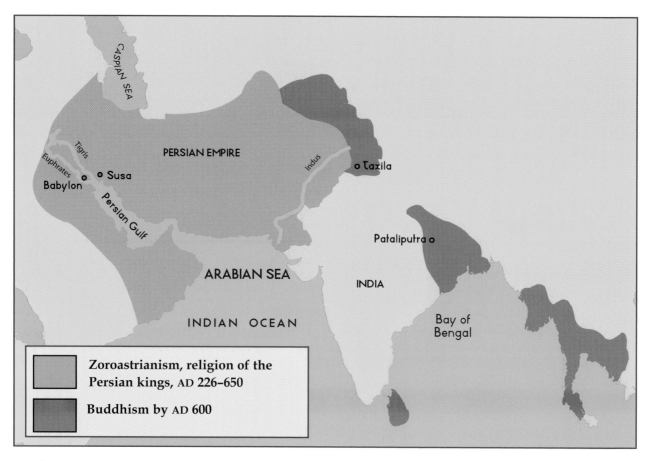

Religions such as Zoroastrianism and Buddhism have a history that dates back to ancient times. Zoroastrianism was founded by the Persian prophet Zoroaster. After his death, nomads carried his teachings throughout the Persian Empire. Buddhism, like Zoroastrianism, originated from one man, Siddhartha Gautama Buddha (586–482 BC), who searched for the solutions to all of life's suffering. Buddhism spread throughout India and Asia from the sixth century BC.

Transoxania and India, establishing the Seleucid dynasty.

The Kushan Dynasty

Over the next centuries, Hsiung-nu tribes from Mongolia overran central Asia, further blending populations and cultures. The Hsiung-nu, a group of Iranian-speaking people, also known as Yüeh-Chih or Tokharians, took over Transoxania, creating the Kushan Empire. The Kushans controlled territory as far east as India and established their capital in what is now northwestern Pakistan. The Kushans flourished on the wealth generated from the growing trade relationships between China and the Roman Empire. The most famous king of this dynasty, Kanishka, promoted Buddhism as the state religion, and, through merchants from Sogdiana, the religion reached China.

2 THE EMERGENCE OF ISLAM

A new people and a new religion entered the complex mix of central Asia in the seventh century AD. Arab armies, recently converted to Islam, conquered the region and incorporated it into the larger Muslim Empire that had already spread from Spain to Persia.

Prior to the growth of the Muslim Empire, however, Transoxania witnessed yet another periodic migration. This movement marked the first time Turkic peoples journeyed from the east, probably Mongolia. These Turkic nomads briefly took control of Transoxania as well as territory right up into Byzantium (Istanbul). They were soon displaced by fresh waves of eastern immigrants as well as invasions by Chinese armies.

In the sixth century AD, an Arab trader named Muhammad spread Islam among the tribes of Arabia. This new religion ended idol worship and established monotheistic ideals in central Asia. Islam shared many beliefs and prophets with Judaism and Christianity and soon spread through the Arabian Peninsula. After Muhammad's death, his successors, known as *khalifas* (caliphs), felt threatened by hostile neighbors such as the Byzantine (Roman) and Persian Empires, and set about conquering neighboring lands. After successes against the Romans and Persians, they set their sights on Marwannahar — Transoxania.

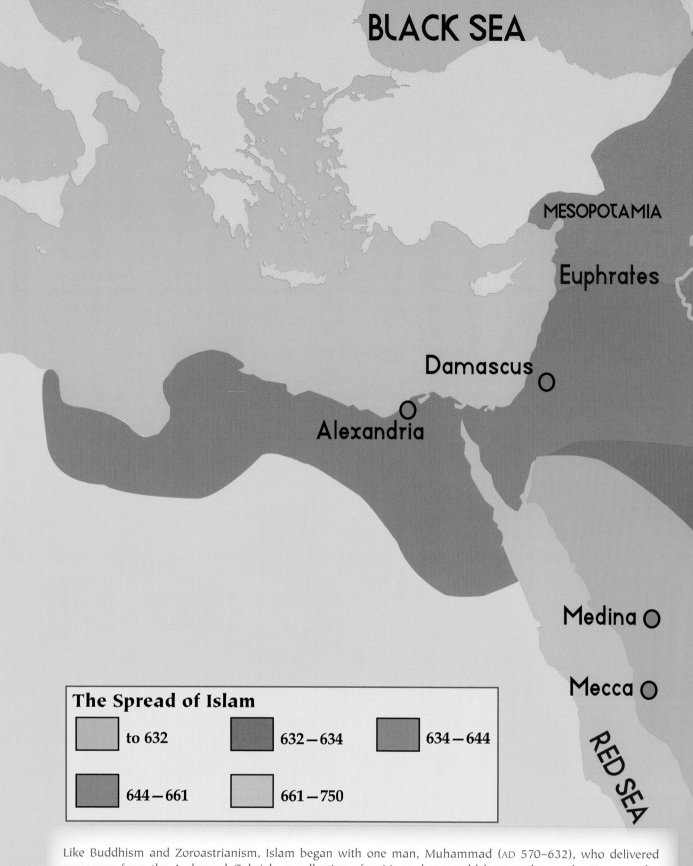

BLACK SEA

MESOPOTAMIA

Euphrates

Damascus ○

Alexandria ○

Medina ○

Mecca ●

RED SEA

The Spread of Islam

▢ to 632	▢ 632–634	▢ 634–644
▢ 644–661	▢ 661–750	

Like Buddhism and Zoroastrianism, Islam began with one man, Muhammad (AD 570–632), who delivered messages from the Archangel Gabriel—a collection of writings that would later make up the Koran—who imparted that Muhammad was chosen as the prophet of Allah, the one God. Islam, like Christianity or Judaism, is a monotheistic religion. Islam spread in every direction after Muhammad's death, and the capital of the Muslim Empire was moved from Medina to Damascus and, finally, to Baghdad.

CASPIAN SEA

Bukhara ○

○ Samarqand
(Samarkand)

Nishapur ○   ○ Balkh

                                      ○ Ghazna

SASSANID EMPIRE   ○ Kandahar

Tigris

Persian Gulf

ARABIAN SEA

Gulf
of Aden

Marwannahar

The Arabs at first made sporadic invasions into Transoxania in the middle of the seventh century AD during their conquest of Persia. At the time, Transoxania was divided among squabbling chieftains and tribes. The Arabs, on the other hand, had an organized, motivated army led by a successful general, Qutaybah ibn Muslim. Qutaybah captured Bukhara in 709, Samarkand in 712, and Ferghana in 715. After some decades of Turkic uprisings and Chinese invasions, the most decisive Arab victory came at the Battle of Talas (Dzhambul, Kazakhstan) in 751. The Arabs defeated the combined local and

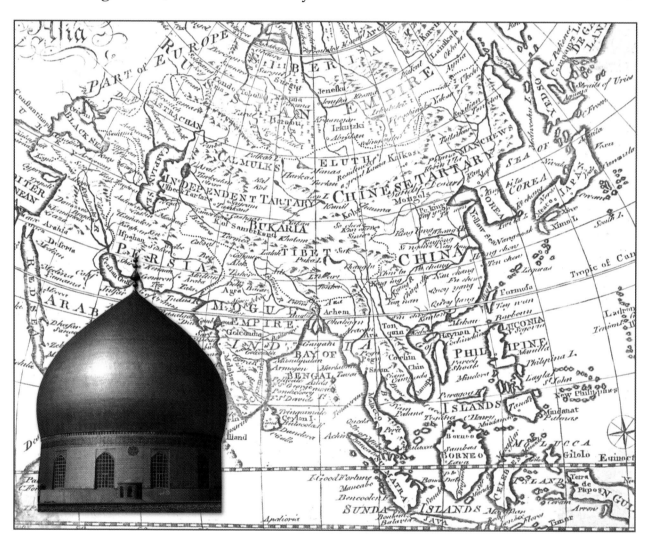

This historical English map of Asia, which features the Mongol and Persian Empires, dates from 1797. The shrine *(bottom left)*, now in present-day Iraq, is the golden dome of the Shrine of Askari in the ancient city of Samarra. Samarra was an Islamic city of the Abbasid dynasty—the Golden Age of Islam—and was built between the eighth and tenth centuries, a time when many Islamic cultural centers were home to the world's greatest scholars and artists.

Chinese armies, ending Chinese ambitions in central Asia. Transoxania was now the largest Islamic-Iranian cultural and religious territory of influence.

Unlike previous invasions, Arab conquest did not lead to an immediate entrance of Arabs into the now Islamic territory. Arabs instead installed provincial governors in the region, each owing his allegiance to the Arab caliph in Baghdad, where the Abbasid dynasty had established itself. Islam began to spread slowly throughout Transoxania. Of the few Arabs who moved into the region, most intermarried and absorbed local customs. In this way, Transoxania retained its Persian culture and language, though the official language of government, literature, and commerce was Arabic until the tenth century.

The Samanid Empire

As the Abbasid caliphate's (kingdom's) hold on its provinces weakened, local governors throughout the Muslim Empire began to assert their freedom. Independent

However mighty, Persian armies were not safe from Muslim forces. This illumination depicting a Persian battle scene once illustrated a medieval manuscript. By Muhammad's death in AD 632, nearly all of Arabia had converted to Islam. Muslim forces soon demanded the surrender of Persia after Arabs seized Syria, Palestine, and Egypt.

Muhammad Bin Musa Al-Khwarezmi

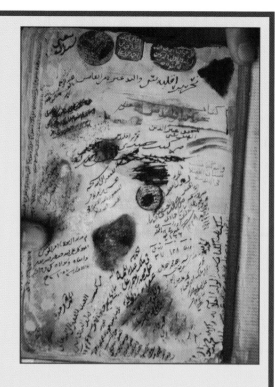

Muhammad Bin Musa Al-Khwarezmi, a native of Khina in Khwarezm, developed mathematical knowledge under royal patronage at the court of the Abbasid caliph Al-Mamun in Baghdad. The word "algebra" is derived from the title of his book, *Al-Jabr wa al-Muqabilah*, a mathematical science unknown in the West until it was translated into Latin during the twelfth century. Al-Khwarezmi developed the decimal system, as well as trigonometric and astronomical tables. The word "algorithm" is derived from his name. Although his date of birth remains unknown, historians have determined that he died around AD 840.

This book, located in the Al-Afqah Library in the town of Tarim in the People's Republic of Yemen, shows Arabic inscriptions in an old manuscript on algebra, the system of mathematics that is marked by its use of letters to represent numbers.

states emerged in Iran and central Asia, paying only slight allegiance to the caliph in Baghdad.

Around AD 850, a Persian dynasty from Bukhara, the Samanids, established themselves in Transoxania, making Bukhara their capital. Historians regard this as the first indigenous (native) Islamic state in the region. Under the Samanids, the Persian language regained its preeminent position as the language of literature and government. The rich and diverse culture of Transoxania flourished, reaching new levels of scientific, cultural, and philosophical achievement.

After the Arab conquest, Transoxania experienced a golden age in literature and learning. Bukhara became one of the leading centers of scholarship, culture, and art in the Muslim world, rivaling other great cities such as Baghdad, Cairo,

Much of the elaborate architecture of the Muslim world is similar to the entrance to the Kalon Mosque in Bukhara, Uzbekistan, pictured here. Besides detailed blue glaze tiles, many mosques also feature passages from the Koran written in a form of Arabic calligraphy. Because Islam forbids the representation of Allah, Islamic art mostly takes the form of intricate designs and patterns and sometimes features Indian-influenced patterns such as floral motifs.

and Cordoba (in present-day Spain). Some of the most renowned historians, scientists, architects, and geographers in Islamic history were natives of the region. Many others traveled there to benefit from royal patronage. The Silk Road facilitated these journeys as Arab merchants traveled back and forth between China, India, and Greece, returning with ancient texts on mathematics, philosophy, and astronomy. Merchants returned with something even more precious from China—the art of papermaking, then unknown to the rest of the world. Armed with paper and books, Arabs translated Greek and Indian works, adding to them their own commentaries and research. Afterward, they made many copies. Kings and princes began assembling huge libraries where they would encourage scholars to study, continuously adding to the knowledge they had acquired.

More Invasions

In the tenth century, a confederation of Turkic tribes known as the Qarakhanids emerged on the margins of Transoxania, north of the Syr Darya. In AD 999, the Qarakhanids, who were also Muslim, defeated the

Avicenna

Ibn Sina (AD 980–1037), known to the West as Avicenna, is famed as the greatest physician of medieval times. He cured the Samanid ruler of Bukhara and received royal patronage. After gaining access to the royal library, Ibn Sina translated works by Aristotle. He systematically collected all medical knowledge into a single book he called the *Qanun fi-al tibb*, or the *Canon*. Ibn Sina, along with Abu Raihan Al-Beruni, is believed to have stolen cadavers on which to conduct experiments. The *Qanun*, in which he discussed human anatomy, established the positions of major organs and the circulatory system. It was translated into Latin during the twelfth century. Later, it became a standard medical textbook in Europe until the 1800s.

Avicenna, featured in this fifteenth-century French manuscript illumination with Guy de Chauliac, a French surgeon, and the Greek physicians Hippocrates and Claudius Galen, introduced the European world to the most advanced medical knowledge of the day.

Abu Raihan Al-Beruni

Abu Raihan Al-Beruni (AD 973–1048) was a traveler, historian, poet, geographer, mathematician, and medic, but he is remembered most for his achievements in astronomy. Centuries before Copernicus, at a time when people believed the world was flat and that the Sun rotated around the earth, Al-Beruni believed the earth was round. He also understood that it rotated on its axis and revolved around the Sun. He plotted the positions of 1,029 stars, accurately estimated the distance to the Moon and the earth's radius, and realized the cause of solar eclipses. He accomplished this without a telescope, an instrument later introduced in 1609 and used by Galileo.

The astrolabe (above) was first developed by Arabs in the ninth century in order to determine positions on land or at sea. The instrument became valuable for Muslims because it was capable of determining the time of day and therefore prayer times, as well as determining the direction of the holy city of Mecca. The astrolabe later became an important instrument for any explorers who crossed vast waterways.

Samanids and took control of Bukhara, formally establishing Turkish control. During this time, there was a continuous flow of Turkic tribes into Transoxania and the rest of central Asia.

During the twelfth century, the Karakhitai, or Khitans, a group of Buddhist tribes originally from either Manchuria or Mongolia, lost their hold over northern China. Driven out, they moved westward across the steppes, overthrowing the Qarakhanids and the Seljuqs, another local Turkic dynasty. They succeeded in establishing an empire stretching from the Aral Sea in the west to the eastern borders of China.

By the early thirteenth century, yet another dynasty emerged in Transoxania. The Khwarezm-shahs had ruled in Khwarezm since the eighth century but always under the authority of the ruling empire. In 1200, Khwarezm-shah Alauddin Muhammad, who was essentially a governor under the Seljuqs, declared himself independent. He then proceeded to conquer territories held by the Karakhitai. Within a few decades, however, the Mongols conquered Khwarezm.

3 FROM GENGHIS KHAN TO TIMUR

A powerful and dreaded force emerged from the east during the thirteenth century, consuming everything in its path. These were the great Mongols, a group of tribes from Mongolia, led by the dynamic and ruthless Genghis Khan, who created one of the largest empires in history.

Genghis Khan

Genghis Khan, also called Chinggis, was born in Mongolia, probably in 1167. His father was a tribal chieftain related to the last khan (king) of the Mongol kingdom. Temüjin, as Genghis was named, was orphaned in his youth. Unable to inherit their father's provinces, Genghis and his brothers grew up as outcasts. Temüjin was later able to form an alliance with other tribes, who elected

MEDITERRANEAN SEA

RED SEA

Mongols arrived in present-day Uzbekistan in 1219, invading its wealthy cities, devastating the region, and killing entire populations. The Turkic Mongol horde settled there and, over time, permanently mixed with the native population. It would take 300 years before the arts and sciences would again flourish in Samarkand, however, and this time it would take place under the leadership of a Mongol descendant named Timur (Tamerlane). Timur would live to conquer present-day Uzbekistan, Iran, Iraq, Syria, and parts of Anatolia.

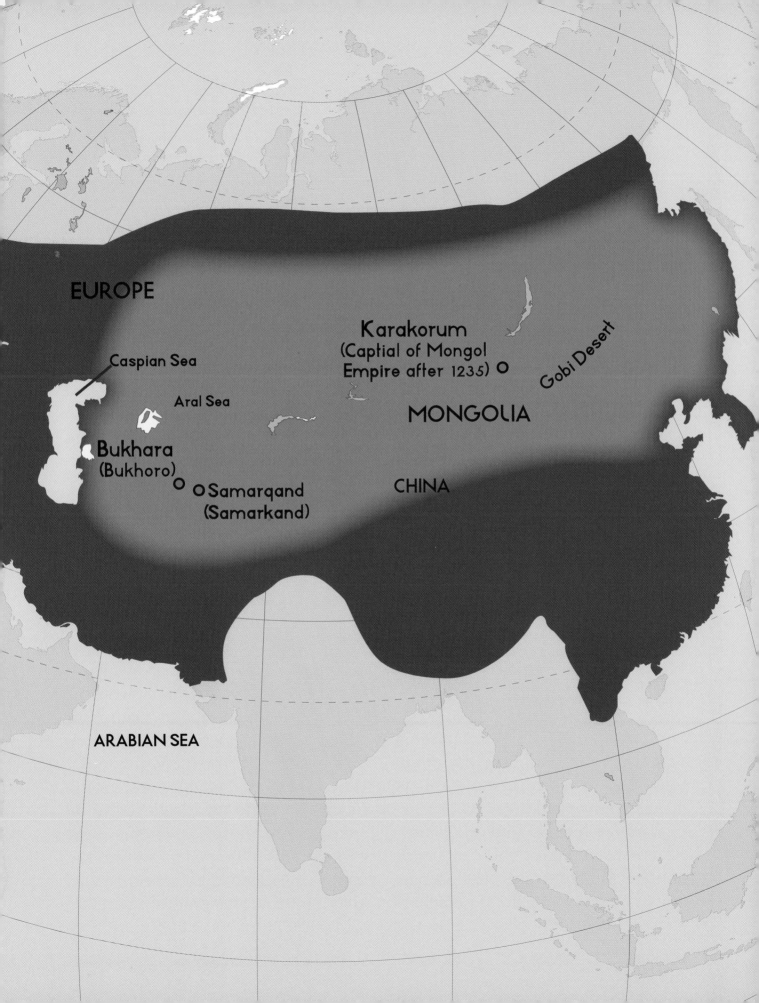

EUROPE

Caspian Sea

Aral Sea

Karakorum
(Captial of Mongol
Empire after 1235) O

Gobi Desert

MONGOLIA

Bukhara
(Bukhoro)

O O Samarqand
(Samarkand)

CHINA

ARABIAN SEA

Rashid ad-Din, a subject of the Mongol court in Persia during the early part of the fourteenth century, wrote a historical account of the Mongol Empire. He also authored the manuscript folio pictured here, featuring Genghis Khan and his four sons, Ögödei, Jochi, Chagatai, and Tolui, in AD 1113. The original is now housed in the National Library of France, in Paris.

sleep in the saddle for days at a stretch. They used this unusual advantage to effectively wreak devastation throughout central Asia. By 1206, Genghis controlled all Mongol lands and called a great assembly of tribal leaders at the River Onon, where he was again named the khan of all Mongols. The once-orphaned outcast had become supreme leader.

Genghis first attacked China, a constant threat to Mongol power, capturing Peking (Beijing) in 1215. Unable to subdue all of China, he instead moved westward, and by 1220 he had taken over Bukhara, Samarkand, Tashkent, and Khojent.

Genghis's conquest of Transoxania was allegedly sparked by the arrogance of the Khwarezm-shah, Muhammad. Genghis had given his protection to a group of Muslim merchants traveling from China through Transoxania. When they reached Khwarezm, the merchants, who were believed to be spies, were killed. Genghis sent envoys to Muhammad to clear the matter, but again, one of the men was killed. Infuriated, Genghis unleashed a Mongol storm on the region. City

him the khan of the Mongols. Temüjin then took on the name Genghis Khan, which some believe means "universal king."

Genghis quickly embarked on a systematic conquest and unification of other Mongol tribes. The Mongol army consisted of skilled horseback archers, reportedly able to ride and after city was sacked. People were killed or forced to serve as advance troops for the Mongols against their own people. Fields and gardens were uprooted and irrigation systems were destroyed as the great khan pursued his revenge against the Khwarezm-shah.

Yasa Law

The Mongols were a diverse group of tribes. Some were pagans, while others were Buddhists and Christians— all religions spread by the Silk Road. All Mongols were governed by the Yasa, the collection of Genghis Khan's maxims, regulations, and instructions. The Yasa was an attempt to preserve the natural resources (for example, water), and the ethical, military, and social structures on which the Mongol's nomadic way of life depended. Here are some of the Yasa laws:

◆ Whoever urinates into water or ashes is to be put to death. No one is to dip their hands into running water, all must use a vessel to draw water.

◆ If in battle, during an attack or a retreat, anyone let fall his pack, or bow, or any luggage, the man behind him must alight and return the thing fallen to its owner; if he does not so alight and return the thing fallen, he is to be put to death.

◆ Whoever finds a runaway slave or captive and does not return him to the person to whom he belongs is to be put to death.

◆ No one is to eat food offered by another until the one offering the food tastes of it himself, even though one be a prince and the other a captive; No one is to eat anything in the presence of another without inviting him to join; no one is to eat more than his comrades, or step over a fire on which food was being cooked or a dish from which people were eating.

The Mongol conquest led to another change in the population of Transoxania. The process of Turkification was consolidated since the khan's armies, though led by Mongols, were made up mostly of Turkic tribes. These tribes had been incorporated as the Mongols moved southward. The Turkic people settled in Transoxania, mixing with local populations, and in the process, made the Iranians a minority.

Over the next decade, Genghis conquered most of eastern Europe and Russia, Iran, the Caucasus, and China, as well as northern India and Afghanistan. His conquests cost an estimated five million lives. This was the first time that a single ruler had united the whole of Eurasia (eastern Europe and central Asia).

Before his death in 1227, Genghis divided his empire into four ulus (segments), later called Khanates.

Eastern Europe, known as the Golden Horde, went to Jochi, his eldest son, while Transoxania and the rest of central Asia was ruled by Chagatai, Genghis's third son. China eventually went to his grandson Kublai, and the heartland of the empire—Mongolia and northeastern Russia—was left to Ögödei, Genghis's second son. In doing so, Genghis established the tradition that only his blood descendants could rule in central Asia and Mongolia.

After the years of death and destruction, a period of relative peace and stability was established. Trade developed further as merchants were able to travel from China, ruled by Kublai, all the way to Hungary, controlled by the Golden Horde, without fearing robbery or attacks or once stepping out of Mongol land. The Mongols also developed *yam*, a horse-relay communication system that was not surpassed in efficiency until the nineteenth century.

The Chagatai khanate controlled the central Asian heartland for the next century. In the mid-fourteenth century, it split into a western and an eastern khanate. The western khanate consisted of Transoxania and most of present-day Afghanistan. The eastern khanate consisted of territory north of the Syr Darya and the Ferghana Valley (now divided between Uzbekistan, Kazakhstan, and Tajikistan).

The Chagatai khans, who ruled from Bukhara, converted to Islam and adopted a Muslim lifestyle, characterized by a more settled existence. In contrast, the eastern khanate, known as Mughulistan ("Land of the Mongols"), maintained ancient nomadic traditions. The western Chagatai rulers realized the benefits of urban dwellings—especially the opportunity to increase their wealth through taxes.

Timur

Near the end of the fourteenth century, a Turkic-speaking Mongol, Timur, gained effective control of the western Chagatai khanate in Transoxania. A skilled horseback archer and swordsman, Timur was born near Kesh and became chief of the Barlas tribe. Timur built his power slowly, first uniting the Turkish and Mongol people in Transoxania and using them to expand his influence into outlying areas such as Khorasan (eastern Iran and western Afghanistan), Khwarezm, Mughulistan, and Russia.

At some point, Timur was injured and developed a limp, earning the name Timur-lang ("Timur the lame"), which Europeans mistook

Timurid Art

Though illiterate, Timur encouraged philosophical debate, scientific study, and great works of architecture. Timur's image of himself is reflected in the grand monuments he commissioned. Samarkand was the heart of his kingdom, and its monuments are the pride of modern Uzbekistan. The first of these was his palace at Shahr-i-Sabz, built around 1380 by masons from Khwarezm. Although it now lies in ruin, a contemporary account of the palace written by Spanish ambassador Ruy Gonzales de Clavijo testifies to its grandeur. Other notable monuments include the Shah-i-Zinda complex and the Bibi Khanum mosque. Timurid buildings are notable for multiple domes and ornate blue tiles. Timur commissioned his mausoleum, the Gur-i-Emir, and the Registan, a massive public square in the heart of the city.

One of the most terrorizing of the medieval conquerors, Timur was said to have treated his subjects brutally, sometimes creating ghastly "towers" out of the heads of his victims. Though he was a ruthless man, he was known to have spared the lives of those individuals who were artistically inclined.

for "Tamerlane." Legend has it that years later Timur caught his attacker and used him for target practice. Timur expanded his empire, annexing Iran, Iraq, eastern Turkey, and the Caucasus region. In 1398, he also attacked Delhi, in northern India, looting its wealth and massacring its population. One year later, Timur attacked the Egyptian Mamluk kingdom in Syria, capturing the Ottoman sultan Bayezid I. He also reached Moscow. Timur liked to name the villages outside Samarkand after the cities he had conquered: Delhi, Cairo, Baghdad, and Damascus.

Timur was never able to take the title "khan" since he was not a direct descendant of Genghis. He instead called himself emir, and later, after marrying the Chagatai khan's widow, gurëgen, or son-in-law. In this way, he maintained the charade that he was a governor under the Chagatai khan, when in reality he was the supreme power. He died in 1405 during one of his campaigns, at Otrar on the Syr Darya, while preparing for an invasion of China.

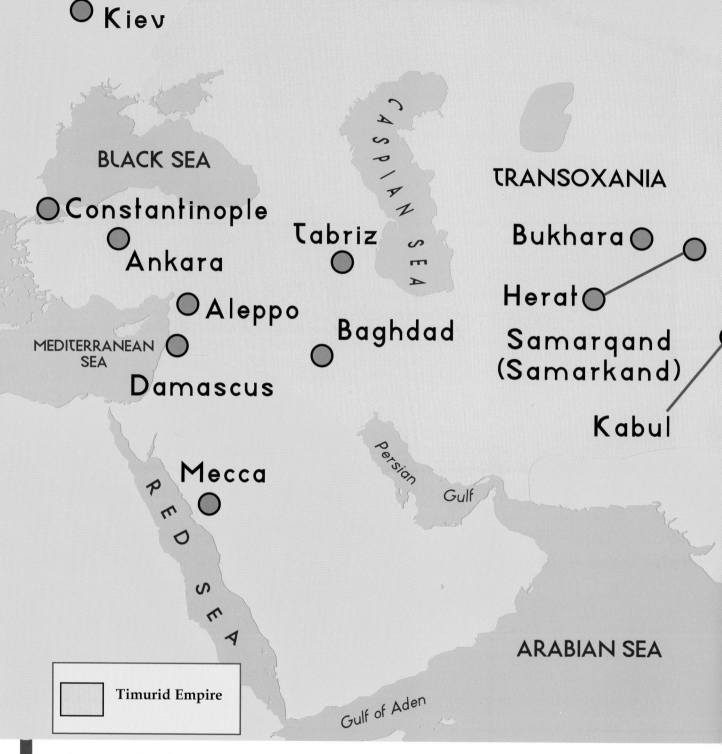

○ Kiev

BLACK SEA

CASPIAN SEA

TRANSOXANIA

○ Constantinople

Tabriz ○

Bukhara ○

○ Ankara

Herat ○

○ Aleppo

MEDITERRANEAN
SEA

Baghdad ○

Samarqand
(Samarkand)

Damascus

Kabul

Persian
Gulf

Mecca
○

RED
SEA

ARABIAN SEA

Gulf of Aden

| Timurid Empire |

Timur swept through central Asia during a thirty-year period, aggressively seizing nearly all of Persia, extending his empire through the north (as far as present-day Moscow) and later, in 1398, through northern India. By 1400, Timur and his armies had entered Syria, defeating forces in Aleppo and Damascus, and Baghdad in 1401. One year later, his forces had reached Anatolia and defeated the Ottoman sultan Bayezid I, seizing Constantinople. But Timur left another legacy behind: During his reign he had gloriously rebuilt Samarkand—a city he had resolved to make the grandest in all of Asia, and one previously razed by Mongol hordes.

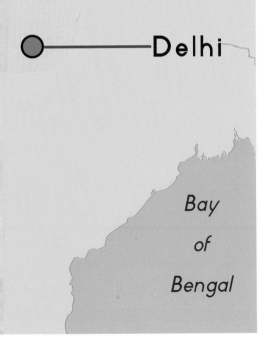

After Timur's death, his sons fought each other for control of his kingdom. Timur's fourth son, Shah Rukh (1404–1447), won. He moved the capital from Samarkand to Herat (now in Afghanistan). Shah Rukh's son Ulugh Beg governed Samarkand from 1409 to 1447, ushering in a new era of peace and prosperity. One of Ulugh Beg's passions was astronomy, and he built an observatory as part of a madrassa in Samarkand's Registan public square. This contribution furthered the city's importance as a center of scientific learning, especially regarding the study of astronomy and mathematics. Ulugh Beg also wrote poetry, composed music, and encouraged the study of history and its documentation. Ulugh Beg was eventually executed on the orders of his son Abdul-Latif in 1449, who resented his father's favoritism of his younger brother.

Within fifty years of Timur's death, his empire crumbled. Like the Mongol dynasty before it, Timur's descendants had divided his territory into small provinces. Of these provinces, Bukhara and Samarkand became the most important. Literature, the arts, and architecture continued to flourish there under royal patronage. It was at this time that Chagatai Turkish evolved as the language of the court and literature. These provinces, however, were in constant rivalry with each other. Because they were unable to combine their strengths against foreign intruders, all of Timur's territories in central Asia were conquered by another wave of nomadic conquests in the late fifteenth century. These successful invasions were led by the Uzbeks.

4 THE UZBEKS AND THE RUSSIANS

The Uzbeks were Turkic tribes from north central Asia, east of the Ural Mountains. They took their name from Öz Beg, a descendant of Genghis's son, Jochi, khan of the Golden Horde. A nomadic people, by the mid-fifteenth century the Uzbeks had migrated toward the Syr Darya from where they launched an attack on the Timurids. Abul Khayr Khan, the Uzbek leader, was killed in battle in 1468. At that time, some Uzbeks moved eastward, joining the Chagatai khan of Mughulistan. The descendants of these Uzbeks were later known as the Kazaks.

The Shaybanid Kingdom

Uzbek offensives continued, and by 1505, Abul Khayr's grandson, Muhammad Shaybani, had conquered Samarkand, Bukhara, and Tashkent. Shaybani was a brilliant military commander and

This detail of a sixteenth-century copper engraving featuring northern Russia was featured as part of an atlas series by Abraham Ortelius. In 1570, Ortelius (1527–1598) became the father of modern cartography by issuing the world's first regularly produced atlas, the *Theatrum Orbis Terrarum*, or *Theatre of the World*. Highly regarded among the most educated men, it soon became the equivalent of a modern-day best-seller and by 1608 was translated into Dutch, German, French, Spanish, English, and Italian.

a poet who traveled with a mobile library. Shaybani died in battle against the Persian king, Shah Ismail Safavi, in 1510, while trying to annex Herat. At the time of Shaybani's death, Uzbeks controlled all of Transoxania, and his descendants established a powerful kingdom based in Bukhara. From there, they attempted to expand into Persia, then controlled by the Safavids. Finally, their attempt continued through Afghanistan and northern India, where Babur, a descendant of Timur, after losing to the Shaybanis, had fled and established the Mughal dynasty.

Peter the Great, pictured here in this engraving from 1710, was a seventeenth-century Russian czar who transformed the nation by introducing social reforms and customs from Western European countries. He also moved the Russian capital to St. Petersburg, a city that he named after himself.

During Shaybanid rule and throughout the seventeenth century, Transoxania and all of central Asia experienced a decline in prosperity. This was because of the decline in trade along the land routes of the Silk Road. This decline was primarily caused by the European discovery of faster sea routes from Europe to Asia by Portuguese and Italian explorers.

By the late 1700s, Transoxania was divided among three Uzbek khanates, each claiming to be descendants of Genghis Khan. These were the Qungrats, based in the city of Khiva; the Mangits of Bukhara; and the Mings in Kokand (Quqon, Ferghana), in the upper valley near the Syr Darya. In the region between the Aral and Caspian Seas, the Turkmens, Turkic people who roamed northern Iran, captured villagers and sold them in Bukhara as slaves.

The constant rivalry between the different khanates, and their lack of modern weapons, was almost an invitation for foreign conquest. This time the threat was from Russian territories in the north.

Russian Imperialism

Until the 1400s, many Russian territories had been under Mongol control. Timur's attacks on the Golden Horde had weakened their hold,

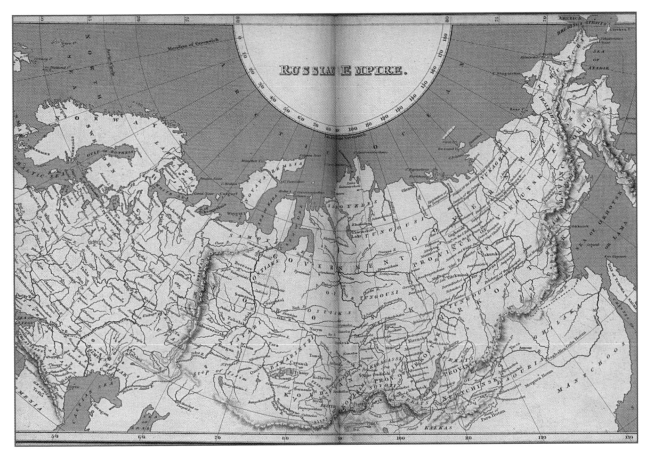

This map of the Russian Empire (1721–1917) was taken from *The Cyclopaedia, or The Universal Dictionary of Arts, Sciences, and Literature*, by Abraham Rees, and shows the empire in 1820. Following the leadership and reforms of Peter the Great, the Russian Empire expanded under the empresses Elizabeth and Catherine the Great, who reigned between 1741 and 1796. Areas of the Ukraine and additional Polish territories were added to the empire during the nineteenth century.

and local Russian princes were able to overthrow the local khans.

The first Russian invasion into central Asia came in 1554. This occurred when the Russian czar, Ivan the Terrible, conquered the Astra-khanid khanate, a Mongol kingdom on the Volga River. The khanate of Sibir (Siberia) was the next to fall, this time to Ivan's son Fyodor. Under Peter the Great, Russia's interest in central Asia developed further. He realized the potential value of the steppes as agricultural land that could boost economic growth in Russia. He was also driven by rumors of gold found in the Amu Darya. In this, he was copying other European powers like England, who had established colonies in Asia, Africa, and the Americas in order to produce less expensive agricultural materials such as cotton and sugar-cane. These materials were then processed into finished goods in factories and sold for profit.

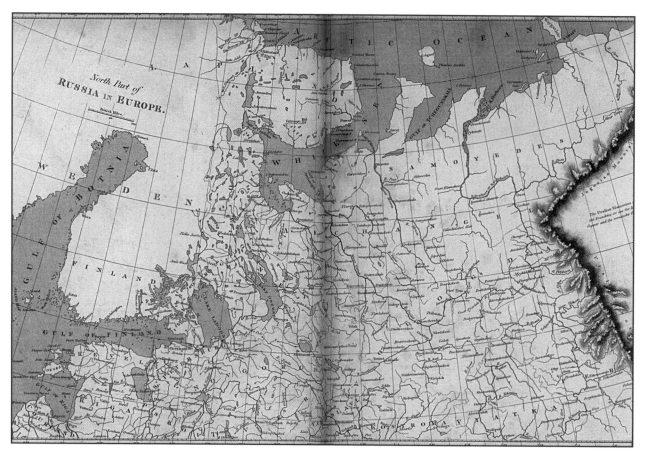

Another view of the Russian Empire in 1820, also by Abraham Rees and also taken from *The Cyclopaedia*, or *The Universal Dictionary of Arts, Sciences, and Literature*. This map, a detail of the northern sections of the empire, shows areas that were either occupied by Russia or under the influence of the Russian Empire, including Sweden, Poland, and Turkey.

By the eighteenth century, Kazakh hordes in Ferghana had accepted Russian independence, and diplomatic relations had been established between the Russian capital in St. Petersburg and the khanates of Bukhara, Samarkand, and Khiva.

The Great Game

The eighteenth century saw the spread of British imperialism in Asia. Britain now controlled nearly all of India and was developing interests in Iran and Afghanistan. The Russians, concerned that the British would soon enter central Asia, wanted to strengthen their borders. The British, on the other hand, believed Russia might advance through Afghanistan and attack India.

In what became known as the Great Game, both countries sent spies and agents into each other's territories, trying to determine exact conditions in central Asia. Both nations also wished to interpret each other's next political move. Traveling under the pretext of hunting trips and scientific surveys, Russian and British spies returned to their countries with stories of exotic kingdoms and great wealth. This information spurred their respective governments into Asia.

In an attempt to stop Britain, Russia annexed Tashkent and Samarkand in 1865. In the next few years, it conquered Bukhara (1868), Khiva (1873), and Kokand (1876), but it allowed the kingdoms to exist

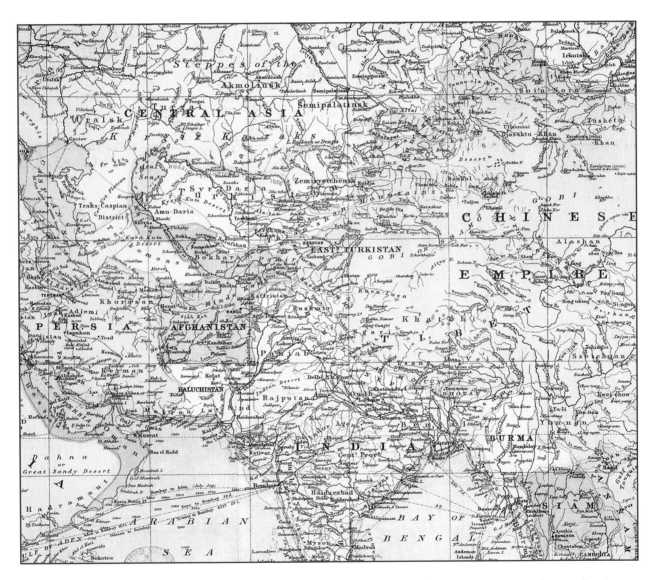

Nineteenth-century competition by rival empires—Imperial Russia and Britain, a country that, at the time, controlled India—became known as the Great Game. Though both countries desired Afghanistan strictly because of its prime geographical location, the British gained more of a foothold there, exerting might over its foreign affairs until the time of Afghanistan's independence in 1919.

This group of Russian peasant women is wearing typical clothing of the period, circa 1900. It was common during that time to wear tunic-like garments made from woolen or silk brocades, with or without sleeves. Most skirts were either knee- or ankle-length, and much of the clothing featured fur or detailed fabric trims.

its capital. A Russian governor-general was appointed over the province, but local khans were used to collect taxes on the czar's behalf. This revenue was then sent to St. Petersburg.

The British, now alarmed at Russia's expansion, seemed prepared for a showdown with the rival Russian power in Afghanistan. Capturing Afghanistan would bring Russia closer to the warm-water ports of the Arabian Sea. The two countries, however, were able to reach an agreement after an Anglo-Russian convention in 1907, effectively ending the Great Game.

as protectorates under Russian authority.

Russia had become the fastest-growing imperial power, expanding at the rate of 87 miles (140 kilometers) per day in the late nineteenth century. With the whole of Transoxania under its control, Russia united the khanates into a single province in 1886, which it called Turkestan, with Tashkent as

Industrializing Asia

Like other imperialist powers, Russia justified its conquests in the name of civility, claiming that Russians were civilizing foreign savages. In reality, Russia now had access to what it called "surplus land"—territory belonging to nomadic tribes—on which it could grow cotton, a natural commodity in high demand domestically and in the international market. Russian cloth factories had depended on raw cotton imported from the United States, but the American Civil War interrupted that supply. During the 1880s, now using central Asian land, Russia was growing enough cotton to meet its own needs, as well as enough to export.

To facilitate the transportation of both goods and people, the Russians built railroads. By 1888, Samarkand and later Tashkent were linked in a railroad network that connected the entire Russian empire. The czar encouraged Russians to migrate into Russian Central Asia, creating enclaves of European settlements in major cities. By 1914, there were 50,000 Russians in Bukhara alone.

The Jadidist Movement

Years of Russian rule bred discontent among the people of Central Asia. This discontent bred a new movement of young middle-class intellectuals who emerged to challenge Russian imperialism. Called the Jadidists, these activists believed that all aspects of Central Asian society had to be reformed, especially aspects that controlled religion, in order to overthrow the Russians. The Jadidist Movement promoted modern education and was marked by a pride in the people's Turkic heritage. It increased pan-Turkic nationalism, or a unified Turkic pride, and made "unity in action, thought, and action" their slogan.

The Jadidists were unsuccessful in their attempt to win independence. However, one of the movement's goals—the overthrow of the Russian Empire—was achieved by another movement: the Socialist Revolution.

This mosque entrance is one part of a larger madrassa, or religious school of Islam, in Samarkand. A madrassa is a specialized institution of learning that was adopted by the Seljuqs to promote Islamic teaching. A madrassa normally houses a central mosque, classrooms, and sometimes lodgings for both students and teachers. By the twelfth century, madrassas had appeared all over the Islamic world.

5 THE SOVIET SOCIALIST REPUBLIC OF UZBEKISTAN

Aral Sea

Muynak

Nukus

Khodzheyli
Keneurgench
Boldumsaz
Yylanly

Urgench

At the turn of the twentieth century, a new political and economic philosophy, Marxism, was gaining popularity in Europe, especially in Russia.

According to Marxism, modern industrial society is based on the exploitation of the working class. Marxists believe this exploitation is caused by the private ownership of property and businesses. Workers toil in factories in extremely poor conditions producing all kinds of goods, but they receive meager wages. Factory owners, in contrast, rake in huge profits. Karl Marx, the founder of Marxism, argued that the cause of this problem was private property, since it corrupted human nature and increased exploitation. He believed that owning property caused people to become greedy for profits at the cost of the workers.

Uzbek, a province of the Union of Soviet Socialist Republics (USSR) from 1924, was mostly directed to specialize in cotton farming, a highly profitable manufacturing export of the USSR. Though the region once had adequate resources for food and was self-sufficient, the switch to the sole production of cotton made it a dependent province, now relying upon outside shipments of grain. Later, the decades of constant farming would deplete vast sections of present-day Uzbekistan, including the Aral Sea.

THE DOGS OF WAR.

Bull A 1. "TAKE CARE, MY MAN! IT MIGHT BE AWK'ARD, IF YOU WAS TO LET 'EM LOOSE!"

These cartoons illustrate the political divisions surrounding Turkey around 1900. The caricature of Russia (*left*) is holding back dogs whose collars name them as the four Baltic states. In the distance is Turkey with its back turned, while a man warns Russia not to threaten the Ottoman Empire. The double-headed eagle of Austria (*right*) is above a man clutching bags of money. To the east is the bear of Russia circling the Black Sea. Britain is depicted as a man straddling the islands of Corfu and Malta and holding the leash of the lion of Egypt.

Marx argued that modern society had reached such a level of industrialization that there was no excuse for poverty or hunger. His solution was a revolution—workers should rebel and overthrow the capitalist system and bring in socialism, in which the state owns everything. Socialism creates the conditions for the last phase, communism, in which all property belongs to everyone, and each person earns as much as he or she needs.

The Russian Revolution

Russia in the early 1900s was marked by an extreme disparity in wealth and poverty. While it had achieved a level of economic development, the economy depended on taxes generated from peasants who worked as farmers. Many intellectuals were troubled by the inequality and suffering that saturated Russian society. They believed that the czar had to be overthrown through a workers' revolution. Under Vladimir I. Lenin, the Russian Marxists, called Bolsheviks, gathered strength in towns and cities. After a failed attempt to take power in Moscow in 1906, they tried again in 1917. This time, the workers succeeded. They formed the Red Army and set up Soviets, Bolshevik committees across the country that took over local governance.

At first the Bolsheviks were critical of the czar's colonies in central Asia and in eastern Europe. They promised that after winning control of the government they would allow self-determination—that is, allow each different region to decide its individual future. Each country would join the new socialist republic or become independent.

The Jadidists in the Russian territory, Turkestan, were greatly encouraged by the Socialist overthrow of the czar. They believed that they would finally gain freedom, but they were wrong. Some Jadidists set up an independent government in Kokand in 1918, which was immediately put down violently by the Tashkent Soviets. Despite opposition from the Jadidists, whom they called the Basmachi, Soviet authorities managed to incorporate Turkestan and the khanate of Khiva into the Soviet Union by 1925.

Hailed as the father of the modern Soviet State, Vladimir Ilyich Ulyanov, known as Vladimir Lenin, founded the Bolshevik party and was a major contributor to the success of the Russian Revolution of 1917. Lenin was fully devoted to the Russian people and a driven political leader who is often quoted as saying, "Revolutions are the locomotives of history. Drive them full speed ahead and keep them on the rails."

Independent Soviet Republics

Soviet authorities in Moscow decided the best way to deal with the discontent in Russian Central Asia was to "divide and rule," a policy used successfully by many imperialist powers. In 1924, Uzbekistan was created as part of a national delimitation that redrew the boundaries of Turkestan, Bukhara, and Khiva into new national Soviet republics. Eventually, they set up

ЗАЕМЪ СВОБОДЫ

ВОЙНА до ПОБѢДЫ

БОРЬБА КРАСНОГО РЫЦАРЯ С ТЕМНОЙ СИЛОЮ.

ПРОЛЕТАРИИ ВСЕХ СТРАН СОЕДИНЯЙТЕСЬ

1ое МАЯ ПРАЗДНИК ТРУДА
ДА ЗДРАВСТВУЕТ МЕЖДУНАРОДНОЕ
ЕДИНЕНИЕ ПРОЛЕТАРИАТА!

СВОБОДА

ТОВАРИЩИ-ДЕМОКРАТЫ
ИВАНЪ и ДЯДЯ СЭМЪ
КИНЕМАТОГРАФИЧЕСКІЙ СПЕКТАКЛЬ ВЪ 7 ЧАСТЯХЪ
ЭТА КАРТИНА ПОСТАВЛЕНА ПОДЪ УПРАВЛЕНІЕМЪ
Г-НА Д.В.ГРИФФИТА

five Soviet socialist republics—Uzbek and Turkmen (1924), Tadzhik (1929), and Kazakh and Kirgiz (1936). Each state had a president and a government similar to the administration that governed Moscow, except that they had to obey policies sent down from Russia's capital. In this way they were able to deal with the Jadidist's ideology of Turkic nationalism and a united Turkestan. Officials promoted minor cultural differences among the Turks of Central Asia and made the Tajiks more aware of their links to Iran. Common histories, languages, traditions, and populations of the area were divided among individual local "nationalities." Some historians have called this process one of ethno-engineering—drawing boundaries and rewriting history to change people's perception of their ethnic identity and background.

At much the same time, communist authorities attempted to eliminate local culture and language through "Russification." People were forced to read and write in Russian to obtain jobs, and the script of the Turkic languages was changed from Arabic to Latin, and later Cyrillic. The government also encouraged Russians to migrate into the region. This migration made the local people a minority in their own land.

One of the beliefs of Marxism is that religion is a false ideology. Marx called religion the "opium of the masses." He believed that religion made impoverished people fatalistic, leading them to believe that their miserable conditions were something God had destined for them. In this way, Russian citizens would not try to change the conditions of their lives since they thought they would be rewarded in heaven for suffering on earth.

Russian socialists tried to erase religion from Russian society—including the colonies—by banning all religious activities. This meant that Muslims, Uzbekistan's religious majority, could not go to mosques, make pilgrimages to Mecca, or learn Arabic. Muslims were even forbidden to own a copy of the Koran. The 25,000 mosques located in Central Asia in 1917 were reduced to only 1,700 by 1942.

These images, all early twentieth-century Russian political posters, emphasize the rise of Russian revolutionaries (*top*), the relationship between Russia and the United States (*bottom right*), and the Socialist (workers) holiday "May Day" (*bottom left*). At the time, Russian intellectuals formed a prolonged resistance movement against Soviet Communism known as the Basmachi Revolt. The emir of Bukhara was ousted in 1920 and replaced with new Jadadist revolutionaries. One year later, however, in 1921, Communist administrators returned.

Johann Baptist Homann, an eighteenth-century German cartographer, designed this map of the Russian Empire. Though it divided in 1917 to form the Russian Soviet Federation of Socialist Republics, and then the United Soviet Socialist Republics in 1922, present-day Uzbekistan would not be fully independent until 1991. Joseph Stalin (*top right*), pictured on a political poster, urged Russia's citizens to oppress any criticism of the controlling Communist government. During his leadership (1928–1953 as totalitarian dictator) he abolished private land ownership and had millions of people killed. These genocidal rampages were later known as the Great Purge.

ДА ЗДРАВСТВУЕТ
ВОЖДЬ СОВЕТСКОГО НАРОДА-
ВЕЛИКИЙ СТАЛИН!

After World War II, however, this policy was softened. The Communist government realized that it could never really remove religion from its citizens' lives. It felt a better policy would be to regulate religion through government committees.

Even worse than its social policies, Russia's economic policies devastated Uzbekistan and the other republics. The Russian government continued to use the new Soviet states to produce agricultural products, which were then processed, and profited from, in Russia. By 1928, Premier Joseph Stalin took away people's land to form collective farms. Now the Russian government controlled the production and sales from those lands, as well as any division of profits made by them. At this time, most people in Central Asia were nomads, and they refused to have the land turned into government farms. For them, it meant the end of their way of life. It is estimated that more than one million nomads lost their lives resisting collectivization, while countless others fled into China.

Like the czarist regime, the Communist government wanted to exploit Uzbekistan's fertile river valleys to produce more cotton. The central government made quotas for cotton production, and local authorities would do anything to meet them—scared as they were of the ruthless Stalin. Stalin had already arrested and executed the Uzbekistan Communist Party president Faizullah Khojayev and other officials, replacing them with handpicked Russian government loyalists. Moreover, many of the local officials, especially the new

Faizullah Khojayev

Faizullah Khojayev (1896–1938) began his political career with the Jadidists. He was soon attracted to the Bolsheviks, though, seeing them as the only hope of overthrowing the czarist regime. He became president of the Council of People's Commissars of Soviet Uzbekistan and pursued a policy of greater independence for the people of Turkestan. He also fought central policies that were turning Uzbekistan into a cotton bowl for Russia, using the slogan "You cannot eat cotton." Stalin was furious. He had Khojayev arrested in 1936 on baseless charges and executed in 1938 after a mock trial. In recent times, Khojayev's importance has been recognized and his father's house in Bukhara has been converted into a memorial.

Communist Party president of Uzbekistan, Sharif Rashidov, were corrupt. They often diverted money meant for Moscow to fund their own lavish lifestyles.

Turning most of Uzbekistan into cotton-producing land had many ill effects. Uzbekistan no longer produced food crops and was forced to depend on imports from other parts of Russia. There were also environmental repercussions. Cotton is a demanding crop, requiring huge quantities of water and sapping the soil of its nutrients. Increasing amounts of water were diverted from the Amu Darya and Syr Darya to irrigate Uzbekistan's crops. When less water reached the Aral Sea over time, it shrunk to half its original size in thirty years.

By the 1980s, the USSR's socialist policies were failing. People were fed up with the total control that the Communist Party, and through it, the government, exercised over their lives. They wanted a more open government system that was responsive to their needs. People began to express their discontent openly, with grave consequences for the Socialist state.

6 | INDEPENDENCE

By 1985, Mikhail Gorbachev, the new Soviet president, decided to address some of the problems that the Soviet Union faced. He introduced reforms known as *glasnost* (openness) and *perestroika* (political and economic reform). Gorbachev hoped these reforms would strengthen the state. The new policies instead led to a more open expression of Soviet discontent and disorder, leading to the collapse of the Soviet Union.

During the next five years, the central government faced increasing opposition from people who wanted change, as well as from hard-liners who believed Gorbachev was too liberal. The hard-liners attempted a coup, which failed. This alarmed others, and one by one the Soviet republics declared themselves independent. Uzbekistan did so on August 31, 1991. An independence referendum (direct vote) in December of that year was passed with a 98.2 percent approval. The former Communist Party president, Islam Karimov, then became head of independent Uzbekistan.

While Uzbekistan was now free from Moscow's control, none of its government personnel changed. Officials who were members of the Communist Party of the Soviet Union remained in power. Only the party name had changed. It became the People's Democratic

This photograph, taken in 1924 outside the Gur-i-Emir Mosque in Samarkand, shows a crowd gathered to hear a reading of a decree from Moscow in which Uzbekistan was officially declared part of the Soviet Union. The enthusiasm would be no less great when Uzbekistan, like many other Soviet Republics, was declared independent in the early 1990s, as Soviet Communism collapsed.

Party of Uzbekistan (PDPU). There was little democracy, as President Karimov maintained a centralized, authoritative government. He did hold elections for the presidency, however, and won 86 percent of the vote. Still, many people felt strongly that those elections were rigged.

The first parliamentary elections were held in 1994, again dominated by the PDPU, as opposition parties like Erk and Birlik were completely banned or suppressed. Economic policies did not change, either. In 1995, Karimov held another referendum extending his term by five years.

Today, Uzbekistan has a reputation as one of the most authoritative governments in central Asia. The government does not allow free expression of speech, freedom of the press, and of religious and political groups. Uzbekistan's human rights record is also among the worst in the region. Subsequently, this authoritative control of expression

Environmental Catastrophe: The Aral Sea

The Aral Sea is nearly completely depleted as a result of Uzbekistan's demand for cotton crop irrigation. Every year, the sea's level drops by more than 3 feet (1 meter), its volume having fallen by 75 percent in the last thirty years. The area of the sea was more than 41,632 miles (67,000 km) in 1962, but today is little more than 20,505 miles (33,000 km). Twenty-four species of fish found in the sea have disappeared, while species of mammals and birds have more than halved. As the sea shrinks, it no longer has a moderating effect on the surrounding climate. Uzbekistan's summers are hotter, its winters are colder, and its cotton production is falling.

Valley, a region that is economically depressed and politically suppressed, the IMU has become increasingly violent. In recent years, it is believed that the IMU has established links with Osama bin Laden's Al Qaeda terrorist organization.

With independence, Uzbekistan lost some of the aid and support provided by the Russian government, but it has managed to remain remarkably stable. It has rich mineral resources, including gold and natural gas, and a strong agricultural base of cotton—it's the fourth-largest producer in the world—as well as vegetable and grain crops. The state still controls much of the economy, though Karimov has instituted a series of reforms aimed at promoting

has led to a rise of small groups of militant youths. These people believe that democratic avenues are closed and the only way to challenge the oppressive regime is through the use of armed violence. Among the militant groups is the Islamic Movement of Uzbekistan (IMU). Emerging from the Ferghana

Mikhail Gorbachev, whose policy of glasnost (a Russian word meaning "openness") was an effort to loosen Soviet control over the Russian people, even to the point of criticizing government decisions. This photo of Gorbachev, Soviet premier and first secretary of the Communist Party (1985–1991), was taken in Moscow in 1987. He was later made president of the USSR in 1990.

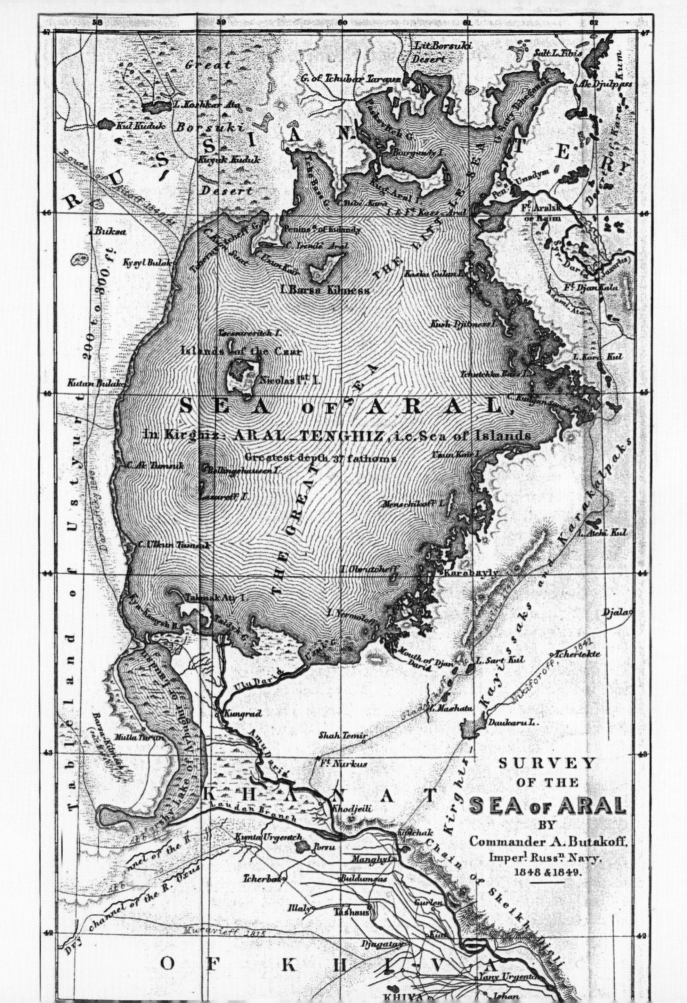

private enterprise. His slow approach has saved Uzbekistan from the situation that other former Central Asian republics have faced; Uzbekistan's gross domestic product (GDP) has fallen only 20 percent, while the central Asian average decline was 50 percent. Still, general living conditions have deteriorated. As wages have fallen, prices have risen, and unemployment is rampant.

Turkic Pride

Recently the Uzbek government has been trying to strengthen national unity by emphasizing the cultural and historical achievements of the Uzbeks. Historical figures are revered, especially Timur, who was once portrayed as a bloodthirsty tyrant by the Soviets. Timur, a Mongol descendant, is now regarded as "father of the nation." In another effort to end Russian influence, the government has made learning the Uzbek language mandatory and is vigorously promoting national culture.

Uzbekistan has been home to many significant minorities over the centuries, notably Russians and Koreans. While many have left the country, the Jewish community based in Bukhara is 50,000 strong and plays an important role in the city's economy and culture.

The Future of Uzbekistan

Many people had hoped that independence would lead to a democratic and free society in Uzbekistan. Instead, the government has continued to use Communist tactics to suppress political and religious expression. Organizations such as Amnesty International and Human Rights Watch, and countries like the United States, have been extremely critical of the Karimov government.

Recently, however, since the September 2001 terrorist attacks on the United States, U.S. policy toward Uzbekistan has changed. The U.S. government now sees the country as a potential ally in its fight against terrorist groups in Afghanistan and the entire Middle East. Uzbekistan is also a potential U.S. economic partner, possessing valuable natural gas located strategically in the heart of central Asia.

Some activists are concerned that U.S. support will give Karimov an

This survey map of the Aral Sea by Commander Alexey Butakoff, of the Imperial Russian Navy, was taken from the *Journal of the Royal Geographical Society* in 1853. The Aral Sea, which derives its name from the Kyrgyz *Aral-denghis*, or the "sea of islands," has been reduced in size to the extent that it is now separated into two parts known as the greater and lesser seas. Though the Uzbek government is now trying to save what remains of what was once the fourth-largest inland body of water, very little can be done to return it to its original grandeur.

opportunity to increase his authoritarian hold over Uzbekistan. They feel that U.S. support will encourage Karimov's aspirations to make the country a regional superpower. In January 2002, Karimov held yet another referendum extending his term, which was to expire in 2005, to 2007 by making the presidential term seven years. Even the United States did not send election observers to the country, explaining that the conditions for a free and fair election in Uzbekistan simply did not yet exist.

Neighboring countries are also wary of Karimov's idea of a greater Turkestan—a confederation of Turkic countries in central Asia—fearing it is a ploy to further Uzbekistan's regional aspirations, maybe even absorb other countries. Uzbekistan is currently involved in border disputes with some of its neighboring states and even sent its

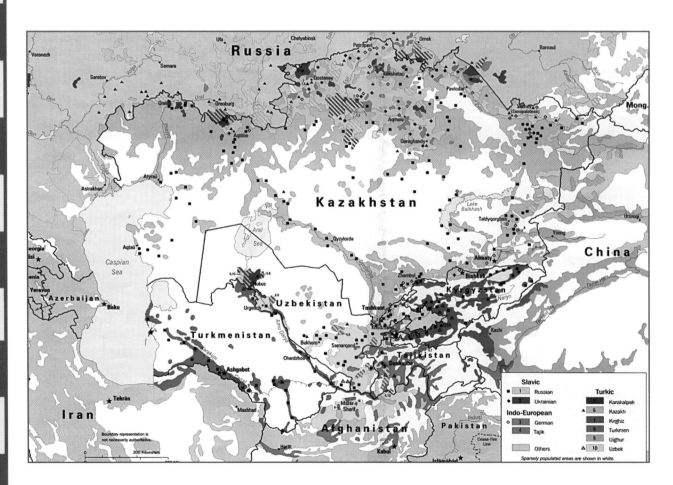

This U.S. Central Intelligence Agency (CIA) map of Uzbekistan and its environs dates from 1993 and details the various ethnic groups that make up its population, then about 22 million people (up to 25,155,064 by July 2001). At the time, about 70 percent of its population was considered Uzbek, as opposed to current statistics, which are up by 10 percent. Presently, about 20 percent of Uzbekistan's residents are of Slavic or Indo-European descent.

This photograph, taken in Samarkand, Uzbekistan, in 2001, shows the view from the interior of a madrassa, a specialized institution of Islamic learning.

troops into Tajikistan during the civil war there in 1992. Of particular interest to those concerned with international human rights and religious freedoms is Karimov's platform to suppress independent Islam in Uzbekistan. In a 2002 letter to U.S. secretary of state Colin L. Powell from Elizabeth Anderson, executive director of Human Rights Watch, the U.S. government was alerted to acts of religious persecution in Uzbekistan. Many of its Muslims have been sentenced to lengthy prison terms for their personal religious practices. In a new era of international fervor to reduce terrorism, Anderson argues that controlling Islamic fundamentalist groups around the world should not become a platform to eliminate Islam or religious freedom. What the future holds for the people of Uzbekistan is uncertain. What remains sure is only Karimov's stranglehold over the country.

TIMELINE

5000 BC Mesopotamia flourishes

3300 BC Writing begins in Sumer

2500 BC Egyptians build the Pyramids

2400 BC Assyrian Empire is established

2334 BC Rule of Sargon I

1750 BC Rule of Hammurabi in Babylonia

638 BC Approximate birth of Persian prophet Zoroaster (Zarathrustra)

600 BC Cyrus the Great establishes the Achaemenid Empire

563 BC Approximate birth of Buddha

331 BC Alexander the Great captures Babylon

323 BC Alexander the Great dies

AD 200 Sassanians rise to power

AD 226 Approximate date Zoroastrianism is reestablished under the Sassanids

AD 313 Christianity is accepted by the Romans

AD 570 Birth of Muhammad

AD 600 Roman, Parthian, and Kushan Empires flourish

AD 610 Muhammad's first revelation

AD 622 Buddhism begins its spread from India to Asia

AD 625 Muslims control Mesopotamia and Persia

AD 632 Death of Muhammad

AD 633–700 Followers of Islam start to spread their faith

AD 685 Shiite revolt in Iraq

AD 750 Abbasid caliphate begins in Iraq

AD 751 Arabs learn papermaking from the Chinese

AD 762 City of Baghdad is founded

AD 1215 Genghis Khan captures China and moves westward

AD 1220 Mongols sack Bukhara, Samarkand, and Tashkent

AD 1258 Mongols sack Baghdad

AD 1379 Timur invades Iraq

AD 1387 Timur conquers Persia

AD 1453 Ottoman Empire captures Constantinople and begins overtaking Asia

AD 1498 Vasco da Gama reaches India

AD 1526 Babur establishes Mughal Empire

AD 1534 Ottomans seize Iraq

AD 1554 First Russian invasion into central Asia

AD 1632 Taj Mahal is built

AD 1739 Nadir Shah invades the Mughal Empire, sacks Delhi

AD 1740 Ahmad Shah Durrani founds kingdom in Afghanistan

AD 1858 British rule is established in India

AD 1932 Saudi Arabia is founded by 'Abd al-'Aziz Al Sa'ud

AD 1947 India declares its independence; East/West Pakistan succession

AD 1985 Soviet leader Gorbachev institutes policiy of glastnost, or openness

AD 1991 Uzbekistan gains independence from the Soviet Union; Karimov becomes president

AD 2000 Karimov reelected president of Uzbekistan

AD 2001 Uzbekistan allows U.S. to use its air bases for strikes against Afghanistan

GLOSSARY

Amu Darya A river in central Asia, called Oxus by the Greeks and Jayhun by Arabs.

Aral Sea A large salt body of water bordered by Kazakhstan and Uzbekistan.

Bukhara A historic city in Uzbekistan that is more than 2,000 years old.

caliphate A territory ruled by a caliph.

central Asia A region composed of Kazakhstan, Kyrgyzstan, Tajikistan, Turkmenistan, and Uzbekistan; located south of Russia, west of China, and east of Iran.

cold war A conflict of ideological differences carried on without full military action, and usually without breaking up diplomatic relationships. A condition of rivalry and mistrust between countries, as with the United States and the Union of Soviet Socialist Republics in the mid- to late twentieth century.

coup (coup d'état) French term meaning "blow to the state," referring to a sudden, unexpected overthrow of a government by outsiders.

Cyrillic The script in which Russian is written.

fatalism Believing that events are fixed in advance for all time and that human beings are powerless to change them.

Gur-i-Emir (Gur Emir) A mausoleum containing the tomb of Timur, his sons, and his grandsons, including Ulugh Beg.

Khanate A territory ruled by a khan, a Mongol lord.

Khiva A city in Uzbekistan, identified with the ancient urban center of Khwarezm.

madrassa A school, usually one where studies are focused on religion.

Marxism The doctrines of Karl Marx on economics, society, and politics. Marx believed that society should be classless, where all property is commonly owned.

monotheistic Religions that worship one god.

Persian One of the major language families spoken in central Asia, which includes Pashto and Tajik.

Samarkand A historic city in Uzbekistan.

Silk Road A series of travel routes that caravans took through central Asia linking China and India to western Europe.

Syr Darya A river in central Asia; also called Jaxartes by the Greeks and Sihun by the Arabs.

Tashkent The capital city of modern Uzbekistan.

Timur (Tamerlane) A medieval king who ruled from Samarkand.

Transoxania The ancient name of Uzbekistan.

Turkic People of Turkic ethnicity; one of the major language families spoken in central Asia, which includes Kazak, Kyrgyz, Turkmen, and Uzbek.

FOR MORE INFORMATION

Asia Society and Museum
725 Park Avenue
New York, NY 10021
(212) 288-6400
Web site: http://www.asiasociety.org/

Association for Asian Studies
1021 East Huron Street
Ann Arbor, MI 48104
(734) 665-2490
Web site: http://www.aasianst.org

Silk Road Foundation
P.O. Box 2275

Saratoga CA 95070
e-mail: info@silk-road.com
Web site: http://www.silk-road.com/
toc/index.html

Web Sites

Due to the changing nature of Internet links, the Rosen Publishing Group, Inc., has developed an online list of Web sites related to the subject of this book. This site is updated regularly. Please use this link to access the list:

http://www.rosenlinks.com/liha/uzbe/

FOR FURTHER READING

Frye, Richard N. *The Heritage of Central Asia from Antiquity to the Turkish Expansion.* Princeton, NJ: Markus Weiner Publishers, 1996.
Sinor, Denis. *Inner Asia: History-Civilization-Languages.* Bloomington, IN: Indiana University Publications, 1969.
Macleod, Calum, and Bradley Mayhew. *Uzbekistan: The Golden Road to Samarkand.* Hong Kong: Odyssey Publications, 1999.

BIBLIOGRAPHY

Akiner, Shirin, Sander Tideman, and Jon Hay, eds. *Sustainable Development in Central Asia.* New York: St. Martin's Press, 1998.
Encyclopaedia Britannica. "Central Asia, History of." Retrieved March 2, 2002 (http://www.brittanica.com/eb/article?eu=114577>).
Encyclopaedia Britannica. "Uzbekistan." Retrieved March 2, 2002 (http://www.brittanica.com/eb/article?eu=129494>).
Erturk, Korkut A. *Rethinking Central Asia: Non-Eurocentric Studies in History, Social Structure and Identity.* Reading, England: Ithaca Press/Garnett Publishing, 1999.
Library of Congress. "Uzbekistan — A Country Study." Retrieved March 5, 2002 (http://lcweb2.loc.gov/frd/cs/uztoc.html).
McChesney, Robert. *Central Asia: Foundations of Change.* Princeton, NJ: Darwin Press, 1996.
Soucek, Svat. *A History of Inner Asia.* Cambridge, England: Cambridge University Press, 2000.
UNESCO (Dari, A. H., et al., eds.). *History of Civilizations of Central Asia. Volumes I–IV.* Paris, France: UNESCO Publishing, 1994.